I'm Feeling... SHY

Published 2012 by
A&C Black
An imprint of Bloomsbury Publishing Plc
50 Bedford Square, London, WC1B 3DP

www.acblack.com
www.bloomsbury.com

ISBN 978-1-4081-7184-4

Illustrations: Christiane Engel
Series consultant: Sally Featherstone

A CIP catalogue for this book is available from the British
Library.

This book is produced using paper that is made from
wood grown in managed, sustainable forests. It is natural,
renewable and recyclable. The logging and manufacturing
processes conform to the environmental regulations of the
country of origin.

Printed in China by C&C Offset Printer Co.

10 9 8 7 6 5 4 3 2 1

I'm Feeling...
SHY

By Lisa Regan
Illustrated by Christiane Engel

Life is full of new people and places. It can make you feel shy when you don't know how to act. Your tummy hurts or you can't talk properly. Sometimes feeling shy can stop you trying something new.

Even grown-ups feel shy sometimes. This book will help you find ways to make the shyness go away. Use those times to try something new and learn what fun it can be.

Your PE teacher asks who can show the class how to skip. You know how – but you're too shy to say.

Watch how easy it is when someone else does it. Tell yourself you can do it the next time the teacher asks.

The doctor needs to ask you about your cough. You try to talk but no words will come out.

The doctor doesn't want to trick you, or make you look silly. She will listen carefully when you feel ready to talk.

Your best friend isn't at school today. How will you
find somebody to play with?

The other children might not know you're feeling all
alone. Look for a person you like and ask if you can
join in their game.

Uh-oh! You're at your friend's house playing, but you really need the toilet and are too shy to ask where it is.

Sometimes you just have to be brave and ask. It's better than having an accident, which would make you feel even worse.

Well done! Uncle Marc has told you what a good swimmer you are – but he has made you feel shy.

Be proud of yourself! It would make you sad if nobody noticed how good you are, so don't be shy when they say nice things.

Your mum has taken you to a party and then gone home. Now you wish she hadn't left you alone.

Join in the next game. Just run around or give your
friend your gift and you'll soon feel part of things.

Gulp! At the supermarket you can't see your parent anywhere. But you're too scared to ask for help.

Your parent will be feeling scared too, so you need to be brave. Find a person who works in the shop and tell them you are lost.

A family friend has called at your house. He says hello and asks you what you're playing, but you're too shy to answer.

You don't need to say many words, but if you say nothing he might think you're rude. Just show him your game and tell him something about it.

Notes for Parents and Caregivers

This series of books has been written to help you to help your child understand that strong feelings are a natural part of life, and that, with help from you, they can learn to manage their own feelings and responses to others.

Feeling Shy is a book to share with your child. It is suitable for children from four years old, but you will still find it useful when your child is much older.

Strong feelings are a natural part of being human, and of developing relationships with others. Your child needs your help as he or she learns to manage their feelings without losing control or self-esteem. When your child feels cross, sad, shy, frustrated, angry, jealous or scared, you will understandably be concerned. But you don't have to wait until there is a crisis in your child's life or relationships before starting to help by reading this book - your child will be able to concentrate much better when they are calm.

Here are some general tips about using this book:

- Don't rush to read this book when your child is distressed. At this time they probably need a hug, a quiet time with you, or a favourite soft toy.

- For the first time, always read the book together, so your child understands what it is about. Then you can leave it for them to come back to in their own time.

- Choose a comfortable place, where you can sit together without being interrupted.

- Avoid distractions (TV, radio etc).

- Choose a calm and quiet time. Bedtime is ideal, as your child will be feeling relaxed, warm and comfy.

- If you have more than one child, read the book as a family. It's best not to single out one child. We all need help with managing our feelings, and brothers and sisters sometimes offer really helpful advice and comments.

- If your child seems bored or troubled by the book, stop and do something else. You could read a different book or talk about what you have been doing during the day.

Using this book

Here are some notes you could follow when reading this book with your child.

Read the title of the book, and look at the cover picture. Tell them that the book is about feeling shy, and the children in the book need their help to stop feeling shy. Even if your child hasn't ever felt shy, it may help them to understand their friends or other children they meet.

Tell your child that everyone feels shy sometimes, and shyness may make you blush, try to hide, run away or cry, and all these responses are quite normal, even for grown-ups. Your child needs to know that there is nothing wrong with these feelings, but it helps to talk about what they could do when they feel shy again.

The first two pages of the book will help you to talk about feeling shy, and some of the physical and emotional effects of shyness. Perhaps you could tell your child about a time when you felt shy (at a wedding, an interview, or meeting an important person), talk about how you felt and what you did.

The rest of the book describes some situations that can cause shyness. As you look at each left hand page, before you read the words, see if your child can spot which child is shy and what is happening in the picture. Say "Who do you think is feeling shy in this picture? How can you tell?"

Before you read the right hand page, ask your child how they could help the shy child by suggesting something they could do or say. Try to be positive about everything they suggest, they may find it difficult at first, and older siblings might be able to help with ideas.

When you have finished reading the book, give your child a hug, tell them they are a good problem solver, and leave the book where they can return to it later.

Sally Featherstone